A Problem Solving Book for Young Talkers

Cara Tambellini Danielson M.A. CCC-SLP

Illustrator: Mary Tambellini

Copyright © 2019 Cara Tambellini Danielson
All rights reserved.

ISBN-13: 978-0-578-45591-4

Message from the author:

I developed this book to help young children build on their problem-solving skills. This book promotes critical thinking skills while also encouraging expressive language skills. I find that children love to interact with books when they are given the time to respond. As you read this book with your child, allow your child to think of an answer. (If they don't want to or aren't able to yet – that is fine too! The more they read this book with you the more they will be able to answer.) As they become familiar with the book, encourage them to think of even more possibilities. For example, if the boy is cold, he could: go inside, or get a jacket, or run around to warm up his body.

Have fun reading!
Cara

Cara Tambellini Danielson M.A. CCC-SLP
caraspeechtherapy.com

He scraped his knee.

What can he do?

Get a bandage.

She is hungry.

What can she do?

Eat a snack.

His room
is messy.

What can
he do?

Clean
it up.

She is
tired.

What can
she do?

Go to
sleep.

He spilled milk.

What can he do?

ABC

Wipe it up.

G H I

Her nose
is runny.

What can
she do?

Get a
tissue.

He is
cold.

What can
he do?

Put on
his coat.

She is lonely.

What can she do?

Play with
a friend.

Made in the USA
Middletown, DE
01 March 2021